February 2013

Valley Cottage Library

110 Route 303
Valley Cottage, NY
10989

www.vclib.org

D1710297

Biofuels

by Geoffrey M. Horn

Science and Curriculum Consultant:
Debra Voege, M.A.,
Science Curriculum Resource Teacher

CHELSEA
CLUBHOUSE
An Imprint of Chelsea House Publishers

Energy Today: Biofuels

Copyright © 2010 by Infobase Publishing

Chelsea Clubhouse
An imprint of Chelsea House Publishers
132 West 31st Street
New York NY 10001

Library of Congress Cataloging-in-Publication Data
Horn, Geoffrey M.
        Biofuels / by Geoffrey M. Horn; science and curriculum consultant, Debra Voege.
                p. cm. — (Energy today)
        Includes index.
        ISBN 978-1-60413-782-8
          1. Biomass energy—Juvenile literature. I. Title. II. Series.
    TP339.H67 2010
    333.95'39—dc22   2009044123

Developed for Chelsea House by RJF Publishing LLC (www.RJFpublishing.com)
Project Editor: Jacqueline Laks Gorman
Text and cover design by Tammy West/Westgraphix LLC
Illustrations by Spectrum Creative Inc.
Photo research by Edward A. Thomas
Index by Nila Glikin
Composition by Westgraphix LLC
Cover printed by Bang Printing, Brainerd, MN
Book printed and bound by Bang Printing, Brainerd, MN
Date printed: May 2010
Printed in the United States of America

Photo Credits: 5: Jutta Klee/Ableimages/Photolibrary; 6: iStockphoto; 10: © inga spence/Alamy; 12: AP Images; 13: iStockphoto; 16: Nigel Pavitt/John Warburton-Lee Photography/Photolibrary; 18: iStockphoto; 19: AP Images; 20: iStockphoto; 23: iStockphoto; 26: Universal Images Group/Getty Images; 27: REUTERS/Prashanth Vishwanathan/ Landov; 29: iStockphoto; 31: AP Images; 32: iStockphoto; 35: iStockphoto; 37: Gavin Parsons/Oxford Scientific/ Photolibrary; 39: AP Images; 40: Courtesy of Algenol Biofuels; 43: LEE SANDERS/NTI/Landov.

10 9 8 7 6 5 4 3 2 1

TABLE OF CONTENTS

Words that are defined in the Glossary are in **bold**
type the first time they appear in the text.

CHAPTER 1

A Growth Opportunity

The world gets its energy from many different sources. In the United States, approximately 85 percent of the energy supply comes from coal, oil, and natural gas. Nuclear power provides another 8 percent. All other sources—including solar and wind energy—add up to no more than 7 percent.

Depending so heavily on coal, oil, and natural gas poses a serious problem. These fuels were formed many millions of years ago. They cannot last forever. Supplies of coal, oil, and natural gas are going to run low. To satisfy the world's growing energy needs, scientists are looking at **renewable** fuels—fuels that cannot be used up. Many scientists believe that **biofuels** may help the world meet this challenge.

What Are Biofuels?

Biofuels are renewable energy sources that come from living things. Some of these fuels have been used for a very long time. For example, have you ever gathered branches to build a campfire? If so, you have already handled one of the oldest biofuels—wood. In many countries, wood is still used daily for cooking and home heating.

Another very ancient biofuel is **dung**. Dung is a common name for animal droppings. If you live on a street where dog owners fail to pick up after their dogs, you probably think of

When you light a campfire, you are using wood, which is one of the oldest biofuels.

dung as a major annoyance or health hazard. Much of the world, however, sees dung as a valued resource. Farmers and gardeners use dung (also called manure) as fertilizer to help crops and plants grow. People in many countries use dried cow dung as a fuel for cooking.

Modern Biofuels

The use of biofuels has expanded beyond these ancient resources. Today, many cars run on **ethanol**, usually blended with gasoline. Ethanol is a form of alcohol. This liquid fuel is made from corn, sugarcane, or other crops. Two of the world's major ethanol producers are the United States and Brazil.

Vehicles can also run on **biodiesel**. This fuel is made from vegetable oils or animal fats. It can be used as a substitute for

Cows on the streets of a city in India. In many parts of the world, cow droppings are used as fuel.

diesel fuel made from **crude oil**. Some drivers have stopped buying diesel at service stations. Instead, their cars and trucks run on used frying oil that they get from restaurants. Country singer Willie Nelson, who is a biodiesel user, says his car smells like French fries!

Scientists are working on advanced ways to make biofuels from grasses and garbage. In a decade or two, whole cities may get their power from giant tanks filled with **algae**. (Algae are plantlike life forms that usually grow in water.) Many experts believe that biofuels will have a growing role in the world's energy future.

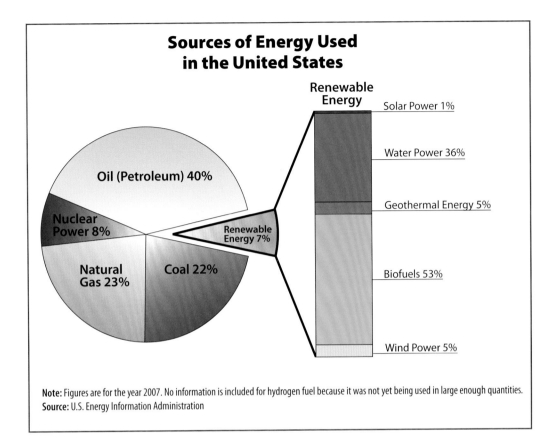

Sources of Energy Used in the United States

Oil (Petroleum) 40%

Nuclear Power 8%

Natural Gas 23%

Coal 22%

Renewable Energy 7%

Renewable Energy

Solar Power 1%

Water Power 36%

Geothermal Energy 5%

Biofuels 53%

Wind Power 5%

Note: Figures are for the year 2007. No information is included for hydrogen fuel because it was not yet being used in large enough quantities.
Source: U.S. Energy Information Administration

Biofuels and Fossil Fuels

Coal, oil, and natural gas are known as **fossil fuels**. *Fossil* comes from a Latin word meaning "dug up." Fossil fuels are the remains of plants and animals that have been dead for many millions of years. The fossil fuels we use today took more than 300 million years to make. They cannot last forever. People are using them much faster than Earth can produce them.

Biofuels and fossil fuels are similar in some ways. Both types of fuel come from living things. The difference is that the supply of fossil fuels will run out. The supply of biofuels will not. Biofuels are renewable. As long as we have sunlight, soil, air, and water, we can always grow more biofuels.

Did You Know?

Running on Sugar

About 200 million people live in Brazil, the largest country in South America. Brazil's living standards are rising. So is the demand for energy.

In the 1970s, Brazil faced a major problem. It was buying about 80 percent of its energy from foreign countries. Most of this spending went for crude oil. The oil was turned into gasoline for cars. This was very costly. Brazil looked for different ways to cut its crude oil imports. One way was to use biofuels for cars instead of gasoline. Brazil was already a major producer of sugarcane. The country used the cane to make sugar, but it could also turn the cane into ethanol—a biofuel that can be substituted for gasoline. Beginning in the 1970s, farmers in Brazil were encouraged to grow more sugarcane. The plan worked. Ethanol output in Brazil has increased a great deal. Now, the nation has little need for oil imports. In addition, Brazil makes money selling ethanol it produces to other countries.

Many companies in Brazil now make what are called **flex-fuel cars**. These cars can run on gasoline, ethanol, or a mixture of the two fuels. These cars sell so well that today, more than four of every five cars sold in Brazil is a flex-fuel vehicle.

The Challenge of Climate Change

A major problem with fossil fuels is their effect on **climate**. When fossil fuels are burned, they produce substances that are called **greenhouse gases**. Greenhouse gases trap heat energy from the Sun. They cause heat to build up in the **atmosphere**. Many scientists say that the buildup of greenhouse gases causes global warming. Global warming poses many different dangers. If climate change continues, for example, some regions of the world may have terrible storms, while other regions will get very little rain. Without enough water, crops will wither and food supplies will run short. This will lead to dangerous **famine**, which will likely hit the world's poor countries and poor people hardest.

Global warming has other effects as well. Ice may melt at the North and South Poles. This would pose dangers to polar bears, who depend on the ice in the Arctic region to live. The melting of the ice would also cause sea levels to rise. As a result, people who live in coastal areas may experience severe floods. In addition, major storms could leave whole cities under water. If current trends continue, major U.S. cities could be in danger. Threatened cities include New York, Baltimore, San Francisco, and New Orleans.

The burning of fossil fuels also causes air pollution. Various substances that are released into the air lead to the formation of smog—an unhealthy mixture of fog, dust, and fumes that can blanket a city. The substances also cause such problems as asthma and lung damage. Fossil fuels have also been linked to acid rain, which has harmful effects on rivers, lakes, crops, plants, and animals.

Did You Know?

E10 and E85

About half of all the gasoline sold in the United States is actually a blend called E10. E10 is about 10 percent ethanol and 90 percent gasoline. E10 is sold at service stations everywhere in the United States. It works well in standard car engines.

A growing number of U.S. filling stations also sell a blend called E85. E85 consists of 85 percent ethanol and 15 percent gasoline. E85 cannot be burned in standard car engines. It can be used only in flex-fuel vehicles. Flex-fuel vehicles make up about 3 percent of the cars and trucks on U.S. roads.

Different kinds of ethanol fuel are available at some service stations.

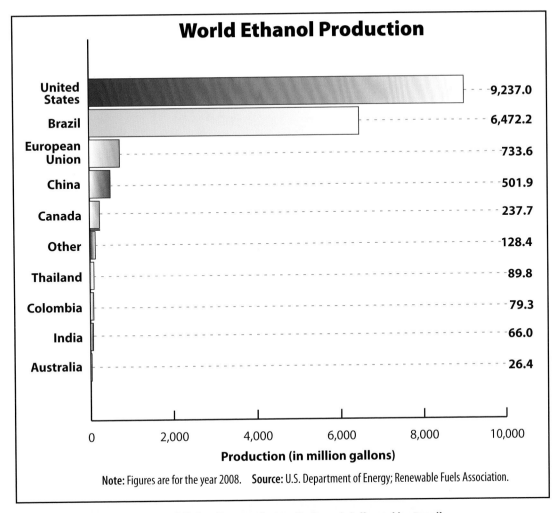

World Ethanol Production

Country	Production (in million gallons)
United States	9,237.0
Brazil	6,472.2
European Union	733.6
China	501.9
Canada	237.7
Other	128.4
Thailand	89.8
Colombia	79.3
India	66.0
Australia	26.4

Production (in million gallons)

Note: Figures are for the year 2008.   Source: U.S. Department of Energy; Renewable Fuels Association.

The United States is the world's leading producer of ethanol, followed by Brazil.

Can Biofuels Help?

Could using biofuels instead of fossil fuels reduce the amount of pollution and the threat of climate change? That depends. Some biofuels used today have serious problems. Like fossil fuels, wood produces greenhouse gases when it is burned. The same is true of ethanol, dung, and some other biofuels.

A major problem with wood is that harvesting too much of it can threaten the world's forests. This can make global warming

Did You Know?

Pop Goes the Biodiesel!

Willie Nelson is not the only star to jump on the biodiesel bandwagon. Film star Daryl Hannah has used biodiesel to run her Chevy El Camino. Singer Melissa Etheridge and the Indigo Girls have used biodiesel to power their tour buses. So have Jack Johnson and Bonnie Raitt. Perry Farrell, lead singer of the group Jane's Addiction, went one step further. On the Lollapalooza tour, he powered whole concerts with biodiesel. Everything—including amplifiers and lights—ran on biofuels.

Folk-rock star Neil Young is an outspoken biodiesel fan. Young drives a sleek, fuel-efficient LincVolt. The LincVolt has the body of an old-fashioned luxury car, the Lincoln Continental Mark IV, but its engine has been retooled. It runs on biodiesel and electric power. Young likes his LincVolt so much he wrote an entire album about it. The album, *Fork in the Road*, came out in 2009.

Willie Nelson prepares to fill his tour bus with biodiesel.

Corn is more than a source of food. It can also be used to produce ethanol, a leading biofuel.

worse, because forests and jungles absorb greenhouse gases. A similar problem happens when jungles are cut down to grow biofuel crops. Farmers in Brazil have cut down some of the Amazon jungle to grow sugarcane for ethanol.

Energy researchers recognize these problems. They are developing new ways to make and use biofuels. These methods would not involve burning. They would not cut down precious forest lands. They would not add more greenhouse gases to the atmosphere. Someday, these new biofuels may help solve both the world's energy supply problem and the problem of global warming.

CHAPTER 2

Nature's Storage Battery

Today, the world gets about 8 percent of its energy from traditional biofuels such as wood and dung. Wood cut for fuel is a very important source of energy in some African countries. Africa as a whole gets more than 20 percent of its energy from wood. In the United States, on the other hand, wood fuel makes up only about 2 percent of the energy supply. About 800,000 U.S. homes burn wood as their main source of heat.

About 2 percent of the world's energy supply comes from modern biofuels such as ethanol. This percentage is likely to increase in the future, as researchers find new ways to replace fossil fuels with renewable fuels.

Understanding Carbon

To understand how biofuels work, you need to understand the **carbon cycle**. The carbon cycle is the process by which living things collect, store, and use energy. Life on Earth could not exist without it.

Carbon is found in all living things. It is also found in the air you breathe and the food you eat. Biofuels contain carbon. So do fossil fuels. In fact, biofuels and fossil fuels are often called carbon-based fuels.

Your body contains carbon along with oxygen and hydrogen. More than 90 percent of the human body consists of these three **elements**. (Elements are the basic building blocks that all things are made of.) Oxygen combines with hydrogen to form water. Water makes up, on average, about 60 percent of body weight. Scientists refer to water as H_2O. This series of letters and numbers is called a chemical **formula**. The formula has a specific meaning. It tells us that water has two parts hydrogen (H) for every one part oxygen (O).

Carbon combines easily with many other elements. These combinations are called **compounds**. Millions of compounds contain carbon. Many of them also contain hydrogen and oxygen. These three elements are all found in ethanol. The chemical formula for ethanol is C_2H_5OH.

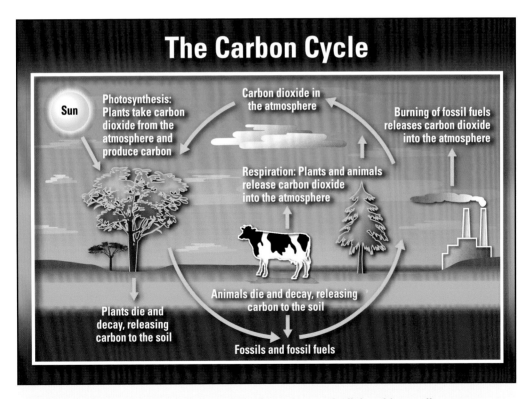

The Carbon Cycle

Sun

Photosynthesis: Plants take carbon dioxide from the atmosphere and produce carbon

Carbon dioxide in the atmosphere

Burning of fossil fuels releases carbon dioxide into the atmosphere

Respiration: Plants and animals release carbon dioxide into the atmosphere

Plants die and decay, releasing carbon to the soil

Animals die and decay, releasing carbon to the soil

Fossils and fossil fuels

Carbon is a key element of life on Earth. In the carbon cycle, living things collect, store, and use energy.

Wood stoves are common in Africa and other parts of the world.

How Plants Store Energy

All living things get energy from the Sun, but simply collecting energy is not enough. Living things also need a way to store energy for later use. Carbon compounds are a key part of this process. They act like a storage battery. They hold energy until it is needed.

At the heart of the carbon cycle is a process called **photosynthesis**. The first part of the word (*photo*) come from the Greek word meaning "light." The second part (*synthesis*) comes from a word meaning "to combine" or "to make." In photosynthesis, green plants and algae take energy from sunlight. They combine this energy with water (H_2O) and **carbon dioxide** (CO_2). CO_2 is a gas found in the air.

Did You Know?

Betting Big
on Biofuels

Companies and countries are spending large sums in the race to develop biofuels. In 2008, for example, new investments in biofuels added up to about $25 billion. The United States, Brazil, China, and India accounted for much of that money.

In the United States, the production of fuel ethanol has grown rapidly in recent decades. In 1981, the United States produced 83 million gallons (314 million liters) of ethanol for fuel. By 2008, the total had increased to more than 9 billion gallons (34 billion liters).

Sugars and Starches

During photosynthesis, plants produce two substances. The first substance is oxygen. It goes back into the air. The second substance is **glucose**. Glucose is a simple sugar. It contains carbon, hydrogen, and oxygen. The word *glucose* comes from an old Greek word meaning "sweet." This form of sugar is found in fruits, honey, and sugarcane. It is also found in the bloodstream.

Glucose is a storehouse of energy. Animals and plants rely on it as an energy source. Animals get glucose by feeding on the plants that produce it. Glucose unites with other elements to make complex sugars and starches. Starches form a major part of the human diet. Rice, potatoes, bread, and noodles all contain starches.

Active children need carbohydrates to give them energy.

Together, sugars and starches are called **carbohydrates**. Carbohydrates are compounds that contain carbon, hydrogen, and oxygen. The first part of the word (*carbo*) means that the substance has carbon. The second part (*hydrates*) means that the hydrogen and oxygen occur in the same proportion as in water. That is, carbohydrates have two parts hydrogen for every one part oxygen.

Energy to Burn

All living things need energy to grow. Animals also use energy to move and keep warm. How do animals unlock the energy stored in carbohydrates? The answer is a process that is called **respiration**.

Did You Know?
Pellet Power

Until recently, biofuels have had a very small part in producing electric power. In 2006, for example, fossil fuels produced about two-thirds of the world's supply of electricity. Renewable energy sources—including sunlight, wind, and biofuels—produced less than 3 percent of the total.

This pattern is changing, and the European Union (EU) is leading the way. Twenty-seven countries belong to the EU. Members include Germany, France, Italy, the United Kingdom, and other major European powers. EU countries have agreed that by the year 2020, 20 percent of their energy will come from renewable sources. To meet this target, EU members will need to produce 20 percent of their electricity from renewable fuels. Power companies in Europe have begun buying large amounts of wood pellets from U.S. companies. Wood pellets look like vitamin pills. They are made from wood wastes such as shredded wood and sawdust. They can be burned in place of coal in electric **power plants**. They can also be used as a fuel to cook food and heat homes.

Wood pellets are a renewable fuel that can be burned in power plants and used to heat homes.

During respiration, animals breathe in oxygen from the air. Oxygen acts like the "on" switch in a flashlight. It turns the energy stored in carbohydrates into usable power. When oxygen is combined with glucose, the glucose breaks down. This process releases energy along with H_2O and CO_2.

Photosynthesis and respiration are like two sides of the same coin. In photosynthesis, green plants take CO_2 out of the air and give back oxygen. In respiration, animals take oxygen out of the air and give back CO_2. The carbon cycle has been going on like this for hundreds of millions of years.

Adding Fuel to the Fire

People's actions affect the carbon cycle. For example, people dig or pump fossil fuels out of the ground. Mining and burning fossil fuels releases carbon that has been locked up in these fuels for many millions of years. This carbon enters the atmosphere as carbon dioxide. CO_2 is a greenhouse gas. The buildup of CO_2 in the atmosphere contributes to global warming.

Coal—a leading fossil fuel—is mostly made of carbon.

As the use of fossil fuels has grown, so has the amount of CO_2 entering the air. In 1980, burning fossil fuels released 18.5 billion metric tons of CO_2. By 2006, more than 29 billion metric tons was released. China burns a great deal of coal in power plants. Between 1980 and 2006, China's output of CO_2 jumped from 1.5 billion metric tons to 6.0 billion metric tons.

Biofuels and Global Warming

Because biofuels come from living things, they, too, contain carbon. This presents a problem. When biofuels are burned, is carbon released into the atmosphere? If so, do biofuels contribute to global warming? Some scientists say no. They believe that burning biofuels instead of fossil fuels can actually reduce the threat of global warming. The explanation for this is based on the carbon cycle.

Biofuel crops use CO_2 as they grow. Biofuels release CO_2 as they burn. As long as people continue to plant biofuel crops year after year, some or all of the CO_2 that is released will be absorbed by the growing plants. The result is that less CO_2 remains in the atmosphere. The more CO_2 that biofuel crops absorb, the less stays in the air to cause global warming.

In Their Own Words

"We will increase our research in...cutting-edge methods of producing ethanol, not just from corn, but from wood chips and stalks, or switchgrass. Our goal is to make this new kind of ethanol practical and competitive within six years."

President George W. Bush, announcing a new biofuel research program in 2006

CHAPTER 3

Waste Not, Want Not

Scientists use the word **biomass** to describe plant matter and animal wastes that can serve as fuel. Biomass comes in many different forms. These include trees, crops (such as corn and sugarcane), grasses, algae and other plants that grow in water, animal wastes (manure), human wastes (sewage), and garbage.

Some forms of biomass can be burned directly. This is true of dry wood branches and twigs. Other forms of biomass need processing before they can be used as fuel. For example, fresh-picked corn cannot be burned in a car engine. Instead, the starch in the corn must be converted to sugar, and this sugar must be turned into ethanol. The ethanol can then be used as fuel in an engine.

Biomass that must be processed is called a **feedstock**. A feedstock serves as raw material. The fuel is the finished product. For example, corn, sugarcane, and grasses can all be used as feedstocks for making ethanol.

A Renewable Resource

A major benefit of using biomass to create energy is that it is renewable. Forests are cut down, but they can be replanted. Crops are harvested, but new crops can be grown. People and animals produce waste daily. People cart a steady supply of garbage to waste dumps everywhere. The world may run out of fossil fuels—but as long as the Sun shines, rain falls, and plants grow, the world will not run out of biomass.

Another major benefit of biomass is that every nation has its own supply. In Brazil and India, for example, the climate favors sugarcane growing. These countries use sugarcane as a feedstock for making ethanol. Sugarcane does not grow well in most of the United States, but corn does. So U.S. ethanol producers use corn as their feedstock.

This gives biofuels another big advantage over fossil fuels. Every country can grow crops that fit its biomass needs. Every country produces wastes and garbage that can serve as a feedstock to produce energy. In contrast, fossil fuels are not

The United States produces millions of tons of trash each year, some of which could be turned into fuel.

Did You Know?
Getting Ethanol from Corn

Ethanol can be made from corn in several different ways. One common method is called dry milling. First, the corn kernels are ground up into flour (or "meal"). Water is then mixed with the meal to make a mash. Next, **enzymes** are added. Enzymes are substances like the ones found naturally in your stomach. They turn the starch in the corn mash into sugar.

Next, yeast is added. (This is like the yeast that bakers use to make bread.) The yeast turns much of the sugar mash into ethanol. The process also produces leftover corn solids and carbon dioxide (CO_2). The corn solids can be dried and used as animal feed. The CO_2 can be sold for use in soft drinks. It can also be used to make dry ice, which is frozen CO_2.

produced in every country. For example, three countries—China, the United States, and Russia—together hold about 60 percent of the world's coal. Most other countries have very little coal or none at all. When they need coal, countries that do not have it must pay a high price to buy it from those that do. The situation is similar with the other fossil fuels—oil and natural gas. Biomass, on the other hand, is produced everywhere.

Turning Waste into Energy

In some countries, people use animal manure as a feedstock. People on farms collect the manure, mix it with water, and put the mixture in an airtight container. This container is called a **digester**. When the manure **decays** (breaks down), it produces **biogas**, which can be used for fuel. Biogas from cow manure is about 60 percent **methane** gas. Methane (CH_4) is a compound of carbon and hydrogen. It burns cleanly and can be used for lighting, cooking, heating, and making electricity. Methane is also the main ingredient in natural gas.

Digesters have been used since the 1950s in Kenya, a country in east Africa. The manure from two cows can supply

Did You Know?
Cutting Oil Import Costs

The United States is a major producer of crude oil. Because the United States uses much more crude oil than it can produce, it is also a major buyer of crude oil from other countries. The nation spent about $453 billion to import (bring in) foreign oil and oil products in 2008. About $335 billion of that total was spent on crude oil. The cost of importing crude oil was almost four times higher in 2008 than in 2000.

One way to cut oil import costs is to substitute biofuels made in the United States. Another way is to conserve energy wherever possible. For example, people conserve energy when they reuse and recycle things instead of buying new ones. They also save energy by using a bike, bus, or train instead of driving their cars. You can help conserve energy right now by turning off lights, computers, and other electronic devices that are not in use.

A biogas digester turns animal waste into biogas, which can be used as fuel.

a farm family with energy for one hour of cooking or five hours of lighting each day. Biogas has also become important in China and India. About two-thirds of Chinese families on farms and in villages rely on biogas as their main fuel.

Human waste can also be used to produce biogas. In U.S. cities and towns, waste and water from toilets is sent through sewer pipes to sewage treatment plants. There, the **sludge** (solid waste) is separated from the dirty water. The water can then be cleaned and treated to make it safe for reuse. This process takes energy. Some sewage treatment plants use the sludge as a feedstock. They convert the sludge into biogas. The biogas is then used as fuel in an electrical **generator**. Electricity from the generator provides power to run the whole plant. This includes cleaning and treating the dirty water to make it safe for reuse.

Did You Know?

Getting Biodiesel
from Weeds

Even plants once thought of as pests can be used as biomass. One such plant is called **jatropha**. Until recently, many people viewed jatropha as a worthless weed. That attitude is changing. The jatropha plant produces seeds containing at least 19 percent oil. When the seeds are crushed, the oil can be removed and used as biodiesel. In car engines, it can replace diesel from crude oil. It can also replace wood in stoves and heaters.

The good news about jatropha is that it can grow in poor soil. It does not need much rain, and it resists bugs and plant diseases. Farmers in Mali, a country in west Africa, have begun planting large amounts of jatropha. In rural areas, it is used as fuel to run grain mills and water pumps. Countries such as China, India, Malaysia, and the Philippines are also planting the crop.

Jatropha must be handled carefully. The seeds are poisonous. People who eat jatropha seeds can get sick. Some experts worry that people who handle large amounts of the seeds may also show ill effects. In addition, jatropha often grows where it is not wanted. If it spreads to fields where food is grown, it could reduce food crop yields.

A woman at work in a jatropha plantation in India.

From Trash to Treasure

Each year, people in the United States throw out more than 230 million metric tons of trash. That adds up to almost three times the amount of garbage Americans got rid of in 1960. What goes into this huge pile of waste? Food scraps and yard trimmings make up part of the haul. The waste also includes product packaging, bottles, clothing, and newspapers. Handled properly, this trash can be a tremendous resource. Grass clippings and some food wastes can be turned into **compost** to help crops

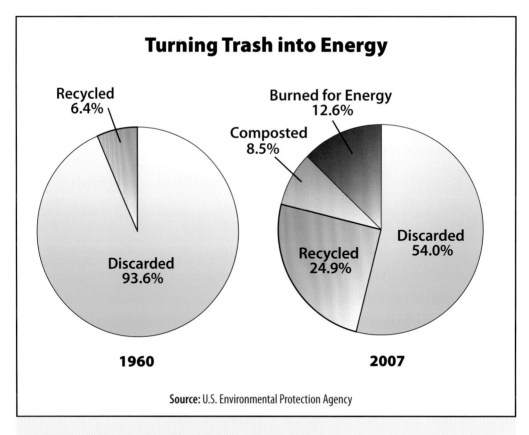

Turning Trash into Energy

Recycled
6.4%

Discarded
93.6%

1960

Burned for Energy
12.6%

Composted
8.5%

Discarded
54.0%

Recycled
24.9%

2007

Source: U.S. Environmental Protection Agency

Americans now make better use of waste. A great deal is now recycled or composted, and a significant amount is burned for energy.

Many food wastes and grass clippings can be turned into compost, which can then be used to help plants grow.

grow. Bottles, plastic items, and paper can be recycled. Some trash can be treated as biomass and either burned or converted to biogas.

Back in 1960, almost no trash in the United States was burned to produce energy. Today, for every eight tons of trash, one ton is burned as fuel. The amount is likely to increase, as more waste dumps find clean, safe ways to burn their trash.

In Their Own Words

"Biomass is the promise and the hope that you don't have to use a food source...to create a greater good. You can use agricultural material that would be thrown away."

Ann Tucker, NatureWorks

CHAPTER 4

Where There's Smoke

As an energy source, biomass has many benefits. It is renewable and can be produced almost anywhere. It can help cut dependence on fossil fuels. It can help countries reduce their import costs for fossil fuels. All this is true. It is not the whole story, however. British researchers have studied many biofuels now used as energy sources. These include biogas, wood pellets, poultry litter, straw, and fuels from energy crops. The scientists found that burning these biofuels released less carbon dioxide (CO_2) than burning fossil fuels. This was good news for people who were worried about global warming.

Other news was not so good. Like fossil fuels, biofuels can cause air pollution when burned. Pollution from nitrogen oxides is a big problem. Nitrogen oxides are gases that contain the elements nitrogen and oxygen. Nitrogen oxides contribute to smog. Nitrogen oxides can also irritate your eyes, nose, throat, and lungs. These gases can make you cough, feel tired, or even feel nauseous.

Black Carbon

Another pollution problem from some biofuels is **black carbon**—the term scientists use for soot. Black carbon can leave a thin layer of dirt and grime on buildings, streets, cars, and clothes. It contributes to smog and is a serious health

Special cookers like this, which use solar power, are a clean, safe alternative to the dung or wood stoves used in many countries.

hazard. Much of the black carbon is produced in Asia and Africa by crude cook stoves that burn wood and dung. Soot and smoke from crude cook stoves cause lung diseases that kill thousands of people each year.

Recent research has shown that black carbon is also a major cause of global warming. Dark particles of soot absorb heat from the Sun. Some of this soot travels through the air and settles on glaciers. This warms the ice and causes it to melt more quickly.

Researchers are developing new types of cook stoves. Some burn biofuels more efficiently. Others use solar power, avoiding biofuels altogether. Widespread use of better cook stoves would reduce pollution, improve people's health, and cut global warming.

Biofuel Costs

In the United States, the government supports the growth of the biofuels industry. A law passed in 2007 requires the production of 36 billion gallons (136 billion liters) of biofuels a year by 2022. At least 15 billion gallons (57 billion liters) of that yearly total will be ethanol from corn. The ethanol will be blended with gasoline.

Currently, it costs more to produce a gallon of ethanol than a gallon of gasoline. To encourage use of biofuels, the U.S. government spends money to keep the price low. Friends of the Earth, an environmental group, reported that the government paid more than $9.5 billion to support biofuels in 2008. The group found that U.S. government support for biofuels could amount to $420 billion between 2008 and 2022.

An ethanol plant in Canada, where corn is turned into automobile fuel.

PEOPLE TO KNOW

VEERABHADRAN RAMANATHAN

Professor Veerabhadran Ramanathan is one of the world's leading experts on climate change. He was born in India and studied engineering and science there. He earned a **doctoral degree** in 1974 from the State University of New York at Stony Brook. He teaches at the University of California in San Diego. Since 2004, he has held the title of distinguished professor of atmospheric and climate sciences.

The problem of soot from stoves has bothered Ramanathan for a long time. When he was growing up, he watched his grandmother cook over wood and dung fires. "After two hours of cooking, she would be coughing like mad," he remembers.

In 2009, he launched Project Surya. (*Surya* means "Sun" in Sanskrit, a language of ancient India.) The project will test cleaner-burning stoves in India. The stoves are designed to produce much less soot.

Fuel versus Food

Is all this spending a good idea? Some scientists do not think so. They are especially worried about ethanol from corn. People eat corn and feed it to farm animals. Corn that is used for fuel cannot be used as food or feed. In addition, growth in ethanol use pushes up demand for corn. That pushes food prices up, too. In recent years, corn prices have risen not just in the United States but around the world. Corn is found in many foods, from breakfast cereals to tacos. When food prices rise, poor people suffer the most.

Ethanol from corn is supposed to reduce demand for fossil fuels. Right now, however, that does not appear to be happening. Farmers who grow corn for ethanol still use large amounts of fossil fuels. Tractors run on diesel from crude oil. So do other farm machines. Fertilizers are made from fossil fuels.

Did You Know?

How Do Biofuels Compare?

Different kinds of fuels are measured in different ways. For example, crude oil is often measured in barrels, coal in tons, and natural gas in cubic feet (or cubic meters). To find which fuels pack the most energy, we need a way to compare them.

In the United States, the energy content of a fuel is often expressed in BTU (or British thermal units). One BTU is defined as the amount of heat needed to raise the temperature of one pound (0.45 kilograms) of water by 1° Fahrenheit (0.56° Celsius). Here is the energy contained in some common fossil fuels and biofuels:

Type of Fuel	Energy Content (in BTU)
SOLIDS	
Coal	20.169 million per ton
Paper pellets	13.029 million per ton
Utility Poles (wood)	12.500 million per ton
LIQUIDS	
Diesel (from crude oil)	139,000 per gallon
Gasoline	124,000 per gallon
Biodiesel	118,300 per gallon
Ethanol	83,330 per gallon
GASES	
Natural gas	1,028 per cubic foot
Biogas (from digester)	619 per cubic foot

Source: U.S. Energy Information Administration

A boy at a county fair enjoys a corn dog—one of many foods that contain corn.

So are the chemicals that kill insect pests. Most of the trucks that carry corn to market still use fossil fuels.

Most of the corn harvested by U.S. farmers is grown in the middle of the country. Most of the ethanol is produced there, too. The ethanol must be carried by tanker trucks or rail cars to the major cities on the East and West Coasts. This also requires large amounts of fossil fuels. In addition, if the truck or train has an accident, the ethanol—which burns easily—may pose a serious fire hazard.

Ethanol crops take land that might be used to grow other food or feed grains. This can also drive food prices up, since farmers may not be planting as many food crops. Ethanol crops also require fresh water, which is scarce in many parts of the world. Some scientists wonder whether the benefits from ethanol are really worth the costs.

Forests in Peril

Another problem with biofuel crops is their impact on forests. For example, Indonesia, a country in Southeast Asia, has become the world's largest producer of palm oil. This oil comes from the fruit and seeds of the oil palm tree. Many foods contain palm oil, which can also be turned into soap. In Indonesia, much of the palm oil is now used as a feedstock to make biodiesel.

To grow oil palms, more than 9.4 million acres (3.8 million hectares) of rain forest have been cut down. From 1996 through 2008, Indonesia lost rain forest at a rate of about 2,000 acres (800 hectares) a day. The effects have been severe. When forest lands are cleared, soils rich in carbon are exposed to the air. They release large amounts of CO_2 into the atmosphere. In addition, the oil palm trees absorb less CO_2 than the dense rain

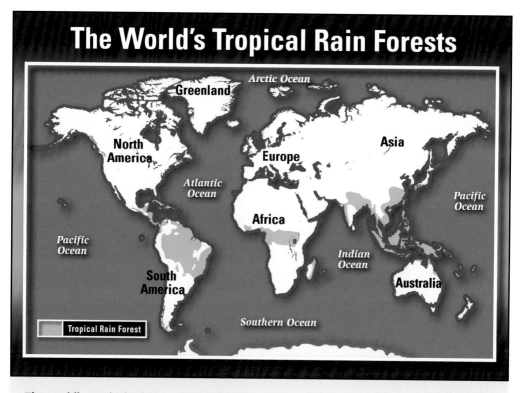

The world's tropical rain forests are disappearing as forests are cut down for the planting of crops, including those used for biofuels.

An oil palm tree growing in Indonesia.

forest they replace. So growing oil palm trees for biodiesel may actually make global warming worse.

Brazil faces a similar problem. The country has already lost a large part of its rain forest. Farmers clear forest land by cutting and burning. This sends large amounts of soot and CO_2 into the air. The forest lands have been cleared by farmers who want to raise cattle, soybeans, and sugarcane. Sugarcane is the main feedstock for ethanol in Brazil. Climate scientists warn that cutting down more rain forest to grow sugarcane could hurt the planet, not help it.

CHAPTER 5

The Future of Biofuels

People have been burning biofuels since ancient times. Today, biofuels are starting to replace fossil fuels for some purposes. Ethanol is burned along with—and in place of—gasoline. Biodiesel is used instead of diesel from crude oil. Unlike fossil fuels, biofuels will always be there when people need them.

Experts believe that in the next few decades, supplies of crude oil will run short. Prices for oil and oil products will go up. For these reasons, the use of biofuels is sure to increase. In addition, more cities and towns will begin to use garbage and sewage as energy feedstocks. If air pollution problems linked to these sources can be solved, this is a very good way to turn mountains of trash into useful energy.

Ethanol from Grasses

How long will people continue to use ethanol? This will depend on whether scientists can find cheap ways to make the fuel from crops that cannot be used as food. Currently, U.S. companies make large amounts of ethanol from the starch in corn kernels. The corn is also needed for food and animal feed. Scientists are working to see if ethanol can be made cheaply from grasses that grow easily and that no one wants to eat.

The answer may involve a substance called **cellulose**. This substance is found in the cell walls of all grasses and trees.

A researcher with a sample of switchgrass, a type of grass that is being studied as a possible source of ethanol.

Cellulose contains carbon along with hydrogen and oxygen. The formula for this carbohydrate is $C_6H_{10}O_5$. Cellulose is complex. It is much tougher to break down than sugars and starches.

Some animals and insects are very good at getting energy from cellulose. For example, termites have enzymes that allow them to eat wood. (This is what makes termites such a problem for people who build and own homes.) The enzymes turn the cellulose into sugar. Scientists already know a great deal about these enzymes. The challenge is to learn how to make large quantities of them at low cost. When this happens, companies will be able to make ethanol cheaply from many different kinds of grasses. This could be very good news. Ethanol from corn yields only about 30 percent more energy than it takes to grow and process the corn. With grasses as a feedstock, the energy gain is up to 80 percent.

Energy from Algae

As a feedstock for ethanol, grasses are much better than corn because they cannot be used for food. Both crops, however, require land to grow on. Another energy crop—algae—is different. It requires no farmland. It does not even need freshwater. Growing in saltwater, algae takes in sunlight and carbon dioxide (CO_2). Algae make large amounts of biomass through photosynthesis. This biomass can be turned into biodiesel and other fuels.

One exciting project, in Venice, Italy, will use biofuel from algae to produce electricity. The algae is grown in large plastic tubes. The CO_2 produced when the fuel burns is not released into the air. Instead, it is pumped back into the tubes to grow more algae. Plans call for the Venice power plant to be finished by 2011.

Many other algae projects are under way. In Florida, for example, chemical companies are building a saltwater "algae farm" to make ethanol. The ethanol would be used as fuel and to make plastics. Another company is growing algae on saltwater ponds in Texas. Algae produces oil, which the company wants to use to make jet fuel.

Algae is being grown in special troughs that are filled with saltwater and covered with plastic.

Did You Know?
From Fries to Fuel

McDonald's has more than 31,000 restaurants in about 120 countries. It is not only the world's largest restaurant chain. It is also the world's biggest seller of burgers and French fries. All those fries are cooked in vegetable oil—millions of gallons of it.

Until recently, restaurant managers threw out all the used frying oil. Now, McDonald's has found a better thing to do with the oil. Today, much of the used frying oil is turned into biodiesel. In Europe, about 80 percent of the used oil becomes fuel. Some of the fuel powers the company's delivery trucks.

More than 7,500 McDonald's restaurants in the United States recycle their frying oil. McDonald's has found a clever way to do this. Each restaurant has separate storage tanks for fresh oil and waste oil. Each week, a large truck stops at the restaurant. The truck pumps in a new supply of fresh oil and collects the waste oil. The waste oil is then sold to a biofuel company. This company refines the used oil, turning it into clean-burning biodiesel.

The Promise of Hydrogen

Recently, scientists have been looking closely at another way of using biomass. All biomass contains hydrogen. Can hydrogen be used to produce energy? The answer is yes. Liquid hydrogen is already used as rocket fuel. Car engines have been designed to run on hydrogen instead of gasoline or diesel.

A shift to hydrogen would be a major step in cutting use of fossil fuels. It could also help reduce global warming. When

LEE LYND

Lee Lynd is a leader in the effort to produce ethanol from cellulose. He holds degrees in life sciences and engineering. In 1987, he joined the faculty of Dartmouth College in New Hampshire. Today, he is a professor at Dartmouth and at the Stellenbosch University, located in South Africa. He is also a co-founder of a biofuel company, the Mascoma Corporation.

Lynd is hopeful about the future of biofuels. He believes that farmers in the United States are prepared to switch from corn to other sources of ethanol.

"The farm community is more ready to listen to ideas about biofuels now than it ever has been," he says. "They don't want to be left out, and if they have to change to new fuels, they'll change."

hydrogen burns, energy is produced along with water. No greenhouse gases are released.

Hydrogen does not exist alone in nature. It is found in many compounds. Water (H_2O) is one such compound. Methane (CH_4)—which is found in biogas—is another. Scientists know how to run an electric current through water to get hydrogen gas. The problem with this method is that it uses a great deal of energy and is very expensive. In addition, scientists know how to get hydrogen by applying superheated steam to methane. This method also has a problem. It releases a gas called carbon monoxide (CO). CO pollutes the air. Breathing CO is a serious health hazard.

Scientists are trying to find a better way to unlock pure hydrogen from biomass. This method would need to be safe and cheap. It would also need to make effective use of the carbon released along with the hydrogen. If scientists succeed in safely turning biomass into hydrogen, they could go a long way to solving the world's energy problems.

Did You Know?

Running on Chocolate

Can you imagine a race car powered by chocolate and steered by carrots? Researchers in England not only imagined it—they built it. In May 2009, scientists at the University of Warwick introduced the "WorldFirst Formula 3 racing car." The car runs on biodiesel that is from chocolate waste and vegetable oils. It is designed to reach racing speeds of more than 145 miles (233 kilometers) per hour.

Scientists also made use of renewable materials in building the car. The steering wheel, for example, includes materials from carrots and other root vegetables. The car body uses materials from potatoes and other plants.

The Formula 3 race car that runs on biodiesel made from chocolate and vegetable oil.

GLOSSARY

algae: Life forms that resemble plants and usually grow in water.

atmosphere: The envelope of air that surrounds the planet.

biodiesel: Biofuels made from plant oils or animal fats that can be substituted for diesel fuel made from crude oil.

biofuels: Renewable fuels that come from living things.

biogas: A gas consisting mostly of methane and carbon dioxide that is produced when biomass decays.

biomass: Plants and animal wastes that can be used as fuel.

black carbon: Soot formed when biomass is burned.

carbohydrates: Compounds consisting of carbon, hydrogen, and oxygen; these compounds, which store energy, include glucose, cellulose, and other sugars and starches.

carbon cycle: The process by which living things collect, store, and use energy. Plants take carbon dioxide from the atmosphere during photosynthesis and return it by respiration; the respiration of animals and the burning of fossil fuels also return carbon dioxide to the atmosphere.

carbon dioxide: A gas formed when fossil fuels are burned; also written as CO_2.

cellulose: A carbohydrate found in the walls of plant cells; also written as $C_6H_{10}O_5$.

climate: The weather and overall conditions in a place as measured over a long period of time.

compost: Decayed plant materials and manure that can be used as fertilizer.

compound: A substance formed when two or more elements unite.

crude oil: Petroleum as it is pumped from the well, before it is refined to make gasoline, jet fuel, and other products.

decay: To break down or rot.

digester: A special container in which manure, mixed with water, is turned into biogas.

doctoral degree: The highest degree, or title, awarded by a university.

dung: Solid waste from humans or animals; also called manure. It can be used as a biofuel when dried, or turned into biogas in a special container called a digester.

element: A basic chemical substance that cannot be divided into simpler substances.

enzyme: A natural substance that can increase the rate at which chemicals react with one another.

ethanol: A fuel that can replace gasoline and is made from crops like corn and sugarcane.

famine: A food shortage severe enough to cause illness or death from starvation.

feedstock: Raw material than can be processed to make biofuels.

flex-fuel car: A vehicle that can run on gasoline, ethanol, or a blend of the two.

formula: In chemistry, a series of letters and numbers showing the elements that make up a compound and the proportions in which they are present.

fossil fuels: Fuels, such as coal, natural gas, or oil, that were formed underground over millions of years from the remains of prehistoric plants and animals. Such fuels are not renewable.

generator: A machine that is used to convert energy, such as that provided by burning fuel or by wind or water, into electricity.

glucose: A simple sugar found in fruits, honey, corn, and animal blood. For plants and animals, glucose is an important energy source.

greenhouse gases: Gases that trap heat from the Sun within the atmosphere; carbon dioxide is one of the most common.

jatropha: A plant that grows easily, even in poor soil, and produces seeds rich in oil. Jatropha oil can be used as biodiesel.

methane: A gas used as a fuel that is the main ingredient in natural gas.

photosynthesis: The process by which plants use energy from the Sun to turn water and carbon dioxide into food; they then give off oxygen. This process is part of the carbon cycle.

power plant: A place for the production of electric power, also sometimes called a "power station."

renewable: A resource that never gets used up. Energy sources such as sunlight, wind, and biofuels are renewable; sources such as coal, natural gas, and oil are nonrenewable.

respiration: The process by which living things take in oxygen and produce energy and carbon dioxide from carbohydrates. This process is part of the carbon cycle.

sludge: Solid waste separated from waste water at a sewage treatment plant. Sludge can be used as a feedstock to produce biogas.

TO LEARN MORE

Read these books:

Armentrout, David, and Patricia Armentrout. *Biofuels*. Vero Beach, Florida: Rourke, 2008.

De la Garza, Amanda. *Biomass: Energy from Plants and Animals*. Detroit: Greenhaven Press, 2006.

Povey, Karen D. *Biofuels*. San Diego: KidHaven Press, 2006.

Solway, Andrew. *Biofuels*. Pleasantville, New York: Gareth Stevens, 2008.

Thomas, Isabel. *The Pros and Cons of Biomass Power*. New York: Rosen Central, 2008.

Walker, Niki. *Biomass: Fueling Change*. New York: Crabtree, 2007.

Look up these Web sites:

BrainPOP: Energy
http://www.brainpop.com/science/energy

EPA Climate Change Kids Site
http://www.epa.gov/climatechange/kids

HowStuffWorks—Alternative Fuels
http://auto.howstuffworks.com/fuel-efficiency/alternative-fuels

Renewable Energy—Biomass
http://tonto.eia.doe.gov/kids/energy.cfm?page = biomass_home-basics-k.cfm

Key Internet search terms:

biodiesel, biofuels, biomass, carbon cycle, climate change, ethanol, greenhouse gases

The abbreviation *ill.* stands for illustration, and *ills.* stands for illustrations. Page references to illustrations and maps are in *italic* type.

About the Author

Geoffrey M. Horn has written more than four dozen books for young people and adults, along with hundreds of articles for encyclopedias and other works. He lives in southwestern Virginia, in the foothills of the Blue Ridge Mountains, with his wife and their five cats. He dedicates this book to Alan, Jonas, Colm, and Sarah Scott-Gleiner.